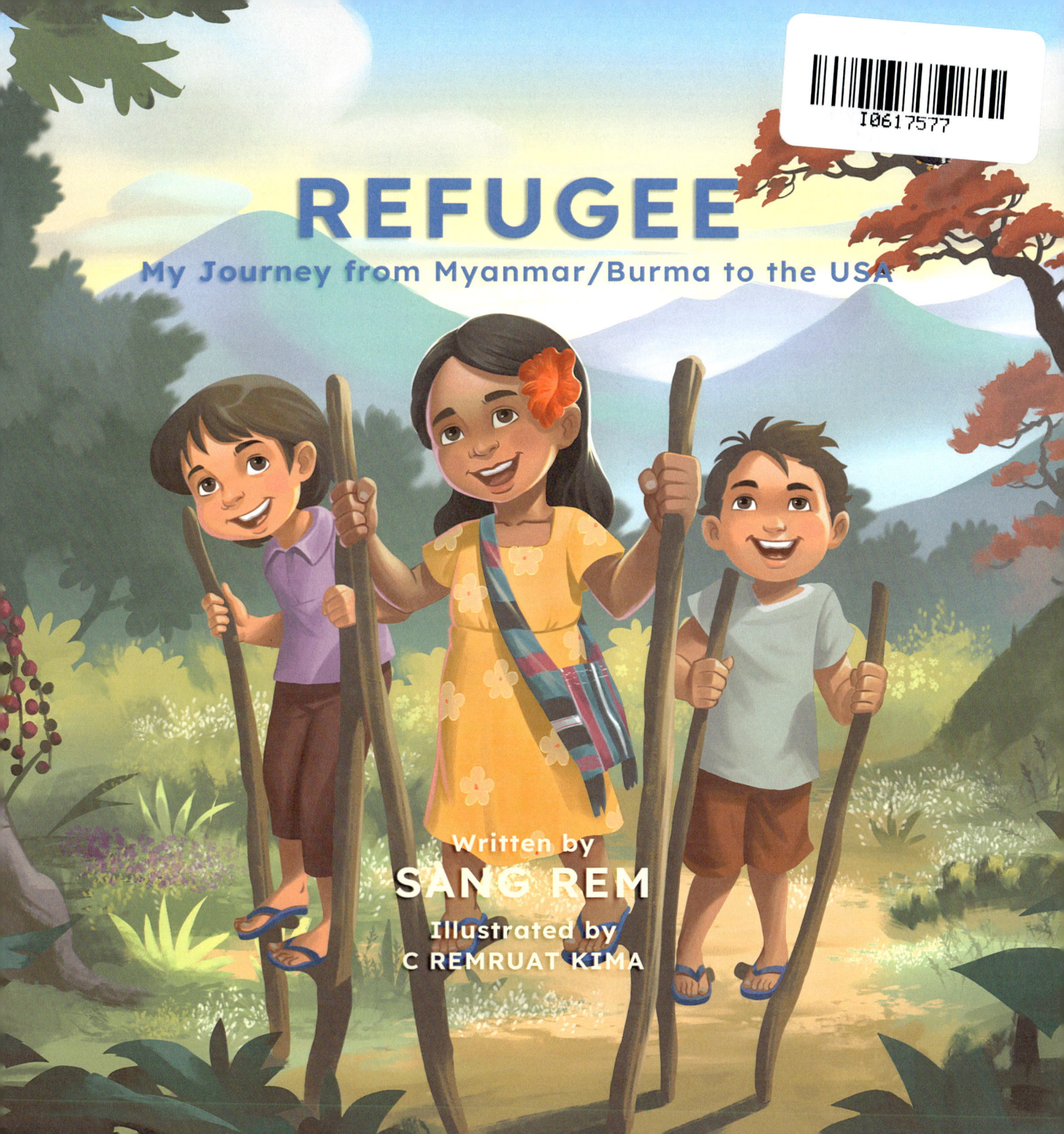

REFUGEE
My Journey from Myanmar/Burma to the USA

Written by
SANG REM

Illustrated by
C REMRUAT KIMA

To all refugees around the world.

Have you ever lived somewhere with tall trees that you can climb endlessly? Have you ever been surrounded by luscious green mountains in every direction? Have you ever known all of your neighbors like a big family?

I was born in a place just like this. This is my story of how I moved from my tiny village in a country called Myanmar all the way to the United States.

Can you find Myanmar on the map at the back of the book?

There are many ethnic groups in Myanmar! Each one has its own unique culture including clothes, foods, languages, religions, and other traditions.

I belong to the Chin ethnic group. We lived in the northwest mountains of Myanmar. There are so many dialects in Chin State. My village spoke the Zanniat dialect.

The Chin tribe is known for gardening, farming, and hunting. We grew corn on the mountains every year! My grandpa also loved growing vineyards around the house.

The most popular Chin meal is corn and vegetable soup. My favorite meal was my grandma's tawh and vegetable dish. I looove tawh! Meals with tawh were extra special because it was hard to find it in the village.

Tawh is rice!

We would split logs in half and create tlau! The water would flow through the tlau, which is how we got water for cooking and taking showers. Trees were used for both enjoyment and everyday purposes.

Growing up, I enjoyed playing on the hills and swinging from the tree branches with my friends and siblings.

I loved my village and all the people who lived there very much. But, there was a war in my country, and it was getting worse. My family needed to move to a safer place. We packed and moved to a city called Kalaymyo.

Everything here was new to us! The land did not have the same rolling hills or luscious green mountains. People who we did not recognize passed by every day. In our tiny village, we knew everyone! My family learned many new things while living in this new culture. We even learned how to cook food in different ways!

I made lots of friends from different backgrounds!

In the city, I learned how to speak Burmese at school.
We also learned the Falam language at church.

During the rainy season, we took showers outside! There was a gutter that sprayed water like a shower head. Sometimes it rained so hard, it hurt our heads!

In our yard, we had all kinds of fruit trees! Some of our fruit trees did not produce enough for all of us, so we would race to get the ripe ones early in the morning!

We also had some animals! I had to watch out for chickens so they would not take my food!

I walked to school every day with my siblings and friends.

Sometimes, we built tents out of huge leaves. Some of the leaves were taller than me! We drew hopscotch in the dirt, played with rocks and sticks, and made dirt cookies.

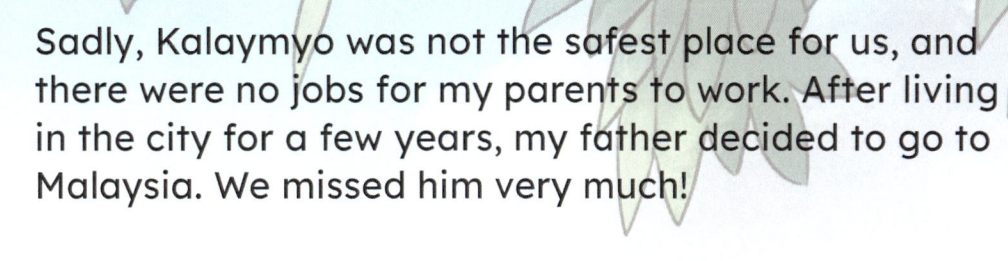

Sadly, Kalaymyo was not the safest place for us, and there were no jobs for my parents to work. After living in the city for a few years, my father decided to go to Malaysia. We missed him very much!

While my father was working in Malaysia, my mom worked hard to take care of us. I enjoyed helping my mom in the garden and the market early in the morning.

Seven years went by while my father lived in Malaysia and the rest of us were still in Kalaymyo. Unexpectedly, we found out some big news. My father had applied to be a refugee with the United Nations, and we were accepted. Our family had to move to Malaysia very fast!

We quit school and said goodbye to our family and friends. It was very sad because we were not sure when we would see them again. While we were sad, we were also brave and began our journey to cross the border.

To stay safe on the border, we could only travel at night. We used boats and cars. We walked and ran. We crossed through rivers, forests, fields, and mud–all without shoes!

We stopped in Thailand to eat and rest before continuing our journey.

Can you find Thailand on the map?

After many years apart, we were finally able to reunite with our father in Malaysia! I knew he had worked really hard in Malaysia for us. We were so relieved to be together again.

Can you find Malaysia on the map?

In Malaysia, we rented an apartment from my father's boss. We were not able to go to school anymore. We played inside every day–singing, drawing, and playing with each other's hair.

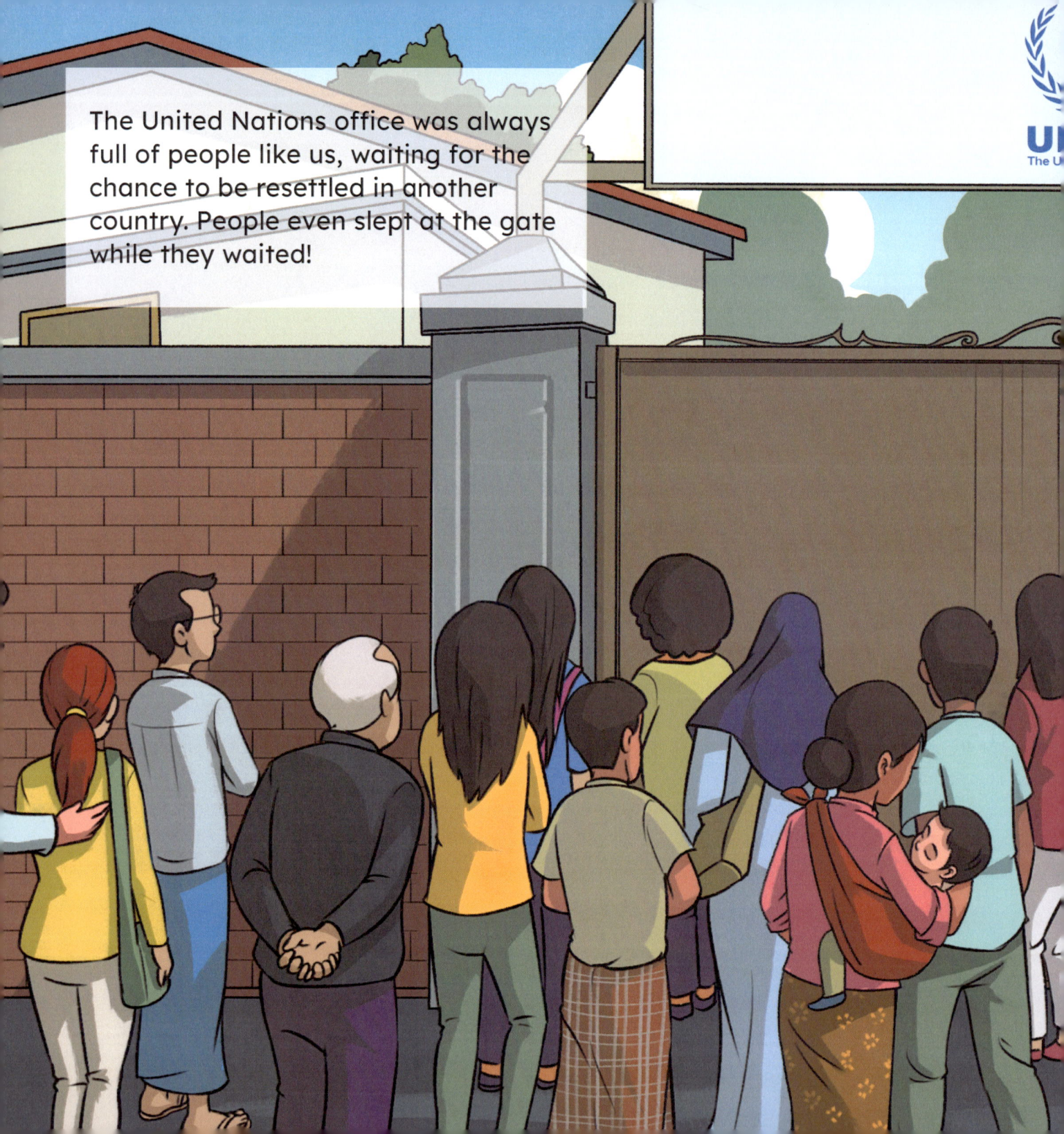

The United Nations office was always full of people like us, waiting for the chance to be resettled in another country. People even slept at the gate while they waited!

It was my first time flying in a plane, and it was a looong flight. We crossed many, many countries.

I wondered what the USA would be like! I had heard that there were big cities with lots of skyscrapers. I was super excited to move to the USA!

Can you find the USA on the map?

We finally made it to the USA! We met new people from all over the world and learned a whole new culture! We were able to go to school again and started learning English. We learned how to cook on a stove, use an air conditioner, and shop with a bank card.

This is my new home! I love meeting new people with different skin colors, cultural backgrounds, and views about life. I enjoy learning about other people's traditions and listening to their stories. My life is full of opportunities to learn new things every day!

I dream about Myanmar all the time and miss my family, friends, and the fresh fruits. I loved living in Myanmar, and I love living in the USA!

WORLD
MAP

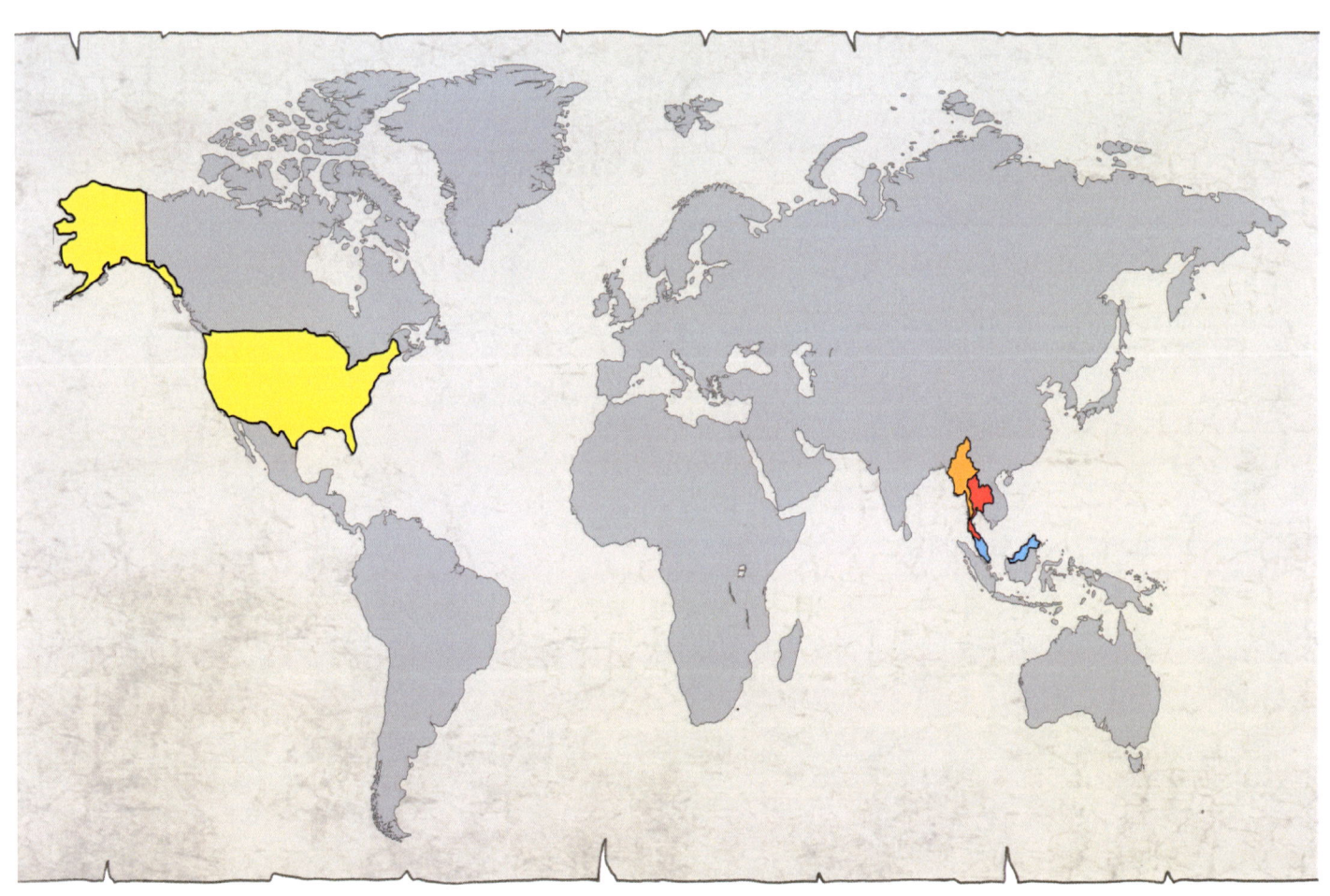

■ United States of America (USA)

■ Myanmar/Burma

■ Thailand

■ Malaysia

MAP OF ASIA

Myanmar/Burma ■

GLOSSARY

Dialects: a form of a language that is used in a local area or by a specific group of people

Myanmar/Burma: a country in Southeast Asia (In 1989, the name of the country changed from Burma to Myanmar.)

Refugee: a person who was forced to leave their home country due to fear

Resettled: to permanently move to a new country after being forced to leave one's home country

United Nations: the organization that aids refugees (United Nations High Commissioner for Refugees, UNHCR)

Zanniat: the language spoken by people of western Myanmar who are a subgroup of the Chin ethnic group

ACKNOWLEDGEMENTS

I feel deeply grateful to my family, friends, colleagues, and professors for their support throughout the process of writing this book. To my dear friend and colleague Makenzie Yeary, thank you for being my biggest cheerleader throughout the entire process of writing this book. To my former professor LaDonna Atkins, Ed.D. and my colleagues Kim Bandy and Kelsey Carroll, Ed.D., thank you for test reading my story. Thank you to my colleague Hannah Bergman for formatting this book. Finally, thank you to my dear friend Abby Cain, M.A. for editing. This book wouldn't be here without all of their support!

AUTHOR
SANG REM

Sang Rem is a former refugee from Chin State, Myanmar/Burma. Sang and her family migrated from Myanmar to Malaysia to the USA from 1997 to 2008. After resettling in Oklahoma, she started learning English as a high school student and went on to complete a bachelor's in Child Development in 2019 and a master's in Family Life Education in 2022 at the University of Central Oklahoma in Edmond. She currently lives in Oklahoma City with her husband Pum Mang and is the Director of Resettlement at The Spero Project.

ILLUSTRATOR
C REMRUAT KIMA

C Remruat Kima received a fine arts diploma from Mandalay Fine Arts School in 2005 and has been working as a digital artist since then. He grew up in the same city as Sang Rem and shares similar childhood memories. With his deep understanding of her experiences, they have worked together seamlessly to create illustrations of this book. Kima currently lives in India due to the oppressive military coup in Myanmar/Burma.